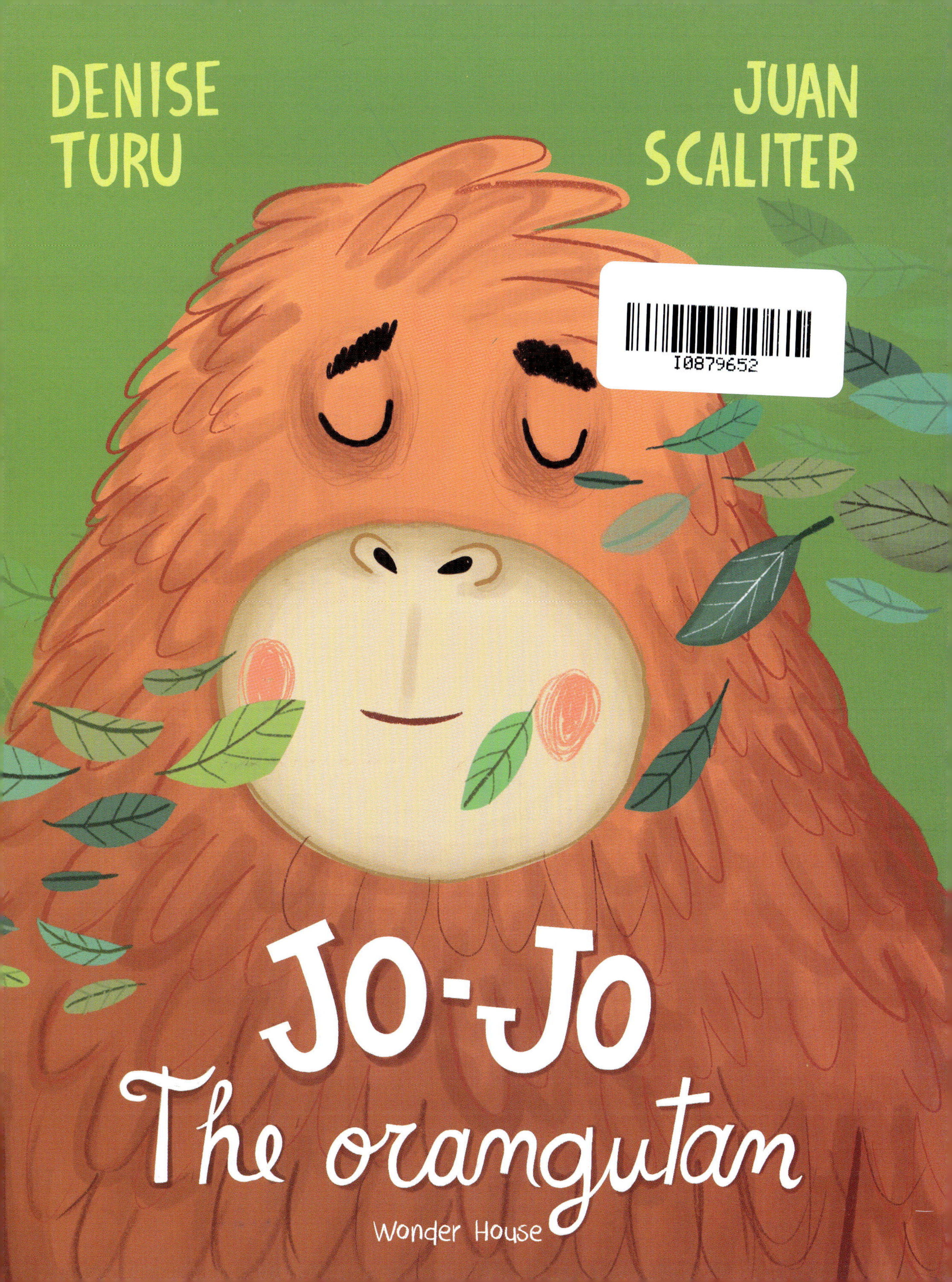
DENISE
TURU
JUAN
SCALITER
JO-JO
The orangutan
Wonder House

Wonder House
(An imprint of Prakash Books)

contact@wonderhousebooks.com

ISBN : 978-93-54404-69-6

JO-JO The orangutan

DENISE TURU | JUAN SCALITER

GREEN IS MY FIRST MEMORY. IT WAS SUCH A BIG COLOR AND I WAS SO LITTLE THAT I OFTEN ASKED MY MOTHER IF SHE COULD HELP ME LOOK AT IT.

THAT'S WHY, WHEN I AM AFRAID OR SAD, I CLOSE MY EYES.
THUS, I SEE WAVES OF LEAVES THAT TAKE ME HOME, TO MY CHILDHOOD, TO MY GREENFANCY.

THE SECOND THING I REMEMBER IS MY MOTHER'S SMELL.
ONE THAT IS NOT SOLD, ONE THAT IS NEITHER MANUFACTURED NOR INVENTED.

IT IS ONLY REMEMBERED AND IF YOU ARE LUCKY, LIKE ME, WHEN YOU CLOSE YOUR EYES, YOU FEEL IT. AND YOU SMILE. SMELLS ARE THE COLORS WE USE WHEN WE WANT TO DREAM.

MY THIRD MEMORY IS ONE THAT I DON'T LIKE, BUT SINCE I DON'T HAVE DRAWERS FOR BAD MEMORIES I HAVE TO WEAR IT ALL THE TIME.

IT IS AN OLD MEMORY, ALMOST AS OLD AS THE PREVIOUS ONES.
BUT SOMETIMES IT TAKES A BIGGER PLACE.

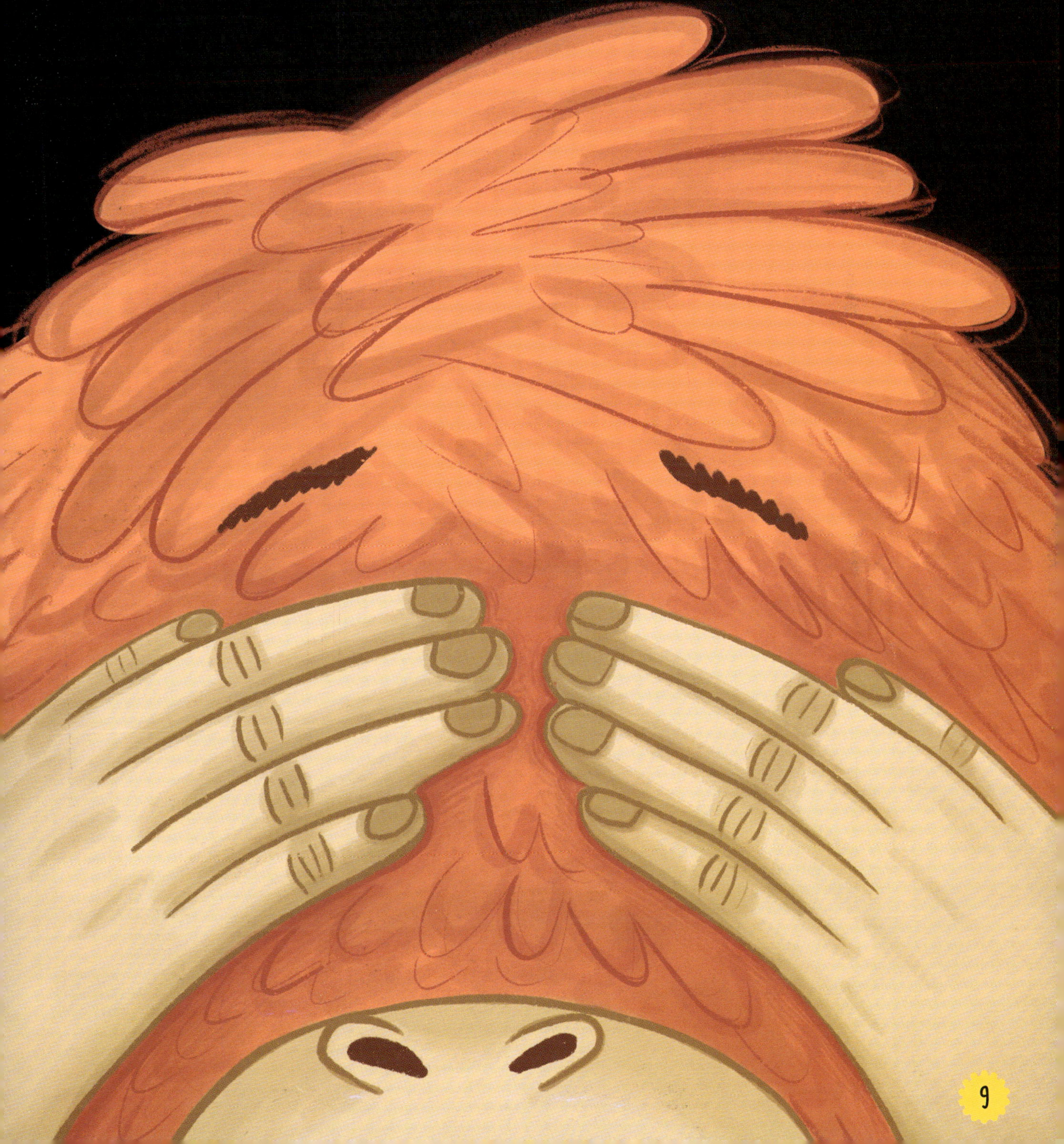

MY NAME WAS NOT ALWAYS JO-JO. WHEN I WAS VERY YOUNG THEY TOOK ME AWAY FROM THE GREEN AND THE COLORS THAT I DREAMED OF. THEY LEFT ME IN A DIFFERENT JUNGLE, WITH UNKNOWN ANIMALS, WITH SMELLS THAT I DID NOT KNOW...

SOMETIMES I WAS AFRAID: I DIDN'T UNDERSTAND THIS NEW JUNGLE AND WHAT I WAS SUPPOSED TO DO TO GET OUT OF THERE. THE STRONGEST TREE IN THE PLACE WAS VERY SMALL, ALL GRAY, ALWAYS COLD AND IT WOULD NOT LET ME GET AWAY FROM IT.

IT HAD VERY TOUGH LEAVES THAT TRAPPED ME. THEY DIDN'T BEND IN THE RAIN AND THEY TASTED AWFUL. AND IF I TRIED TO MOVE THEY HURT ME. IT WAS A SAD FOREST, WITH SAD LEAVES THAT SURELY MISSED GREEN.

I DID LIKE RAINY DAYS. THE EARTH WAS CLEAN, THE WIND FELL ASLEEP IN THE TREES AND I FELT THAT EACH DROP WAS A LETTER TO ME, WITH MY NAME ON IT. AND I DRANK THEM ALL.

BUT, WHEN IT STOPPED RAINING, SOME ANIMALS WOULD COME.
I GAVE THEM CLEAN WATER TO DRINK,

BUT THEY NEVER WANTED IT AND THEY GRUNTED VERY STRANGELY,
AS IF THEY WERE ANGRY. I NEVER KNEW WHY.

THUS PASSED THE RAINS OF FAT DROPS AND LONG NIGHTS. I WAS STILL TRAPPED BY THE LITTLE GRAY TREE AND I COULDN'T MOVE. I STARTED TO FEEL SAD AND FORGET ABOUT THE GREEN AND THE PERFUME. I JUST WANTED TO SLEEP.

BUT ONE DAY SHE CAME. SHE WAS A RARE ANIMAL. SHE LOOKED LIKE THOSE WHO DID NOT WANT MY WATER, BUT APPROACHED VERY SLOWLY, WITHOUT GROWLING.

SHE SHARED SOME WATER WITH ME,
LOOKED ME IN THE EYES (SHE SAW ME!)

AND BROKE THE CHAINS OF THE GRAY TREE.

SHE HUGGED ME AND TOOK ME AWAY FROM THAT FOREST WHICH I HAD NEVER LIKED.

BUT SHE... I DID LIKE HER.
SHE SMELLED GREEN.

SINCE THEN, ANOTHER TEN RAINS OF FAT DROPS AND LONG NIGHTS HAVE PASSED.

NO ONE GROWLS AT ME ANYMORE AND SHE CALLS ME JO-JO.
SHE CARESSES ME AS IF I WERE A LEAF AND SHE IS THE WIND.
SHE DOESN'T SMELL LIKE MY MOTHER, BUT SHE COULD.

NOW I LIVE IN A NEW JUNGLE.
I NO LONGER HAVE TO CLOSE MY EYES TO REMEMBER.

MY STEPS MAY NEVER TAKE ME FAR, BUT MY STORY,
THE ONE I TELL EVERYONE WHO WANTS TO HEAR IT,

THAT STORY TRAVELS AROUND THE WORLD.

WHY ARE ORANGUTANS IMPORTANT?

WHEN DENISE AND I WERE BORN, THERE WERE ALMOST 300,000 ORANGUTANS IN THE WORLD. NOW THERE ARE LESS THAN 100,000. THAT MEANS THAT SINCE YOUR FATHER OR MOTHER WAS BORN, EVERY TWO HOURS, AN ORANGUTAN HAS DISAPPEARED. WHAT HAPPENED? ORANGUTANS *(A NAME THAT MEANS JUNGLE–MAN IN BAHASA, THE LANGUAGE SPOKEN IN INDONESIA)* LIVE IN THE JUNGLES OF BORNEO AND SUMATRA. MOST OF THE RAINFORESTS THERE ARE DISAPPEARING AT A RATE EQUAL TO A FOOTBALL FIELD EVERY 6 SECONDS. THE PROBLEM IS THAT ORANGUTANS NEED LARGE AREAS OF FOREST TO LIVE. BUT THE JUNGLE ALSO NEEDS THEM.

ORANGUTANS ARE KNOWN AS THE GARDENERS OF THE JUNGLE. THEY FEED ON BETWEEN 100 AND 150 DIFFERENT TYPES OF FRUITS AND AS THEY TRAVEL THROUGH THE JUNGLE, FROM TREE TO TREE, THEY SCATTER THE SEEDS THROUGHOUT THE JUNGLE, MAKING SURE THAT THERE IS A LOT OF DIVERSITY AND THAT ALL PLANTS AND TREES HAVE A CHANCE TO GROW. AND ALMOST ALL THE SPECIES THAT LIVE IN THE JUNGLE FEED ON THESE PLANTS. SO, IF IT WEREN'T FOR ORANGUTANS, MANY OTHER ANIMALS WOULD HAVE A VERY DIFFICULT LIFE.

THESE COUSINS OF OURS *(WE SHARE 96.4 PER CENT OF OUR GENES)* HAVE JUST ONE BABY EVERY 5 YEARS AND THEY STAY WITH THE CUB FOR ANOTHER FIVE YEARS. THEY TEACH THEM WHICH TREES TO EAT, HOW TO CLIMB THE BRANCHES AND TO AVOID HUMAN PLANTATIONS, BECAUSE THERE THEY TREAT ORANGUTANS LIKE A PLAGUE AND SEPARATE MOTHERS AND CHILDREN. BUT ORANGUTANS HAVE NO OTHER OPTION. IF WE OCCUPY MORE AND MORE FORESTS AND DO NOT GIVE THEM ROOM TO LIVE, THE ONLY OPPORTUNITY THEY HAVE TO FEED THEMSELVES IS ON THE PLANTATIONS.

WHAT CAN WE DO?

ONE OPTION TO HELP ORANGUTANS IS TO ENSURE THAT WHAT WE EAT DOES NOT HAVE PALM OIL BECAUSE THE FARMS WHERE IT GROWS ARE MAINLY RESPONSIBLE FOR THE DEFORESTATION OF THE FORESTS WHERE THE ORANGUTAN LIVES.

JO–JO LIVES WITH KARMELE LLANOS IN AN ORANGUTAN PROJECT SHELTER. THERE THEY TAKE CARE OF THE ORANGUTANS WHO HAVE BEEN KIDNAPPED FROM THE JUNGLE AND TEACH THEM, AS THEIR MOTHERS WOULD DO– HOW TO RETURN AND REGAIN FREEDOM. THERE ARE ALREADY MORE THAN 200 ORANGUTANS SAVED AND EVERY DAY THEY TAKE IN AND CARE FOR MORE OF THEM.

This is me when I was rescued

Karmele, the woman who helped me.

today I'm 21 years old!!